Ampersand Books
St. Petersburg, FL

All material © 2012 Benjamin Lowenkron
All rights reserved

No part of this this book may be reproduced by any means, mechanical or electronic, without the express written consent of the publisher, except for short passages excerpted for review and academic purposes.

ISBN 978-0-9887328-6-5

Cover design by Matthew Revert.

Typesetting by Robert Hamilton.

Typeset in IM Fell. The Fell Types are digitally reproduced by Igino Marini; www.iginomarini.com.

The publisher would like to thank Eric Elliott, Carrie Causey, Guy Genovese, Michelle Horsley, and especially Jessica Haeckel of Gemiinii Riisiing.

Table of Contents

Preacher - 9

Bone River - 9 | Preacher - 10 | Fire Line (Sermon 1) - 12 | Flight Pattern - 13 | Like Gravity - 14 | 3:08 a.m., Haifa - 15 | Stanford & Lee - 16 | Vidalia - 17 | The Commute - 18 | Evacuated - 19 | Ramona's Spiders (Sermon 8) - 20 | Waterborn - 21 | Terminal Three - 22 | Bring Me My Heart on New Year's Eve - 24 | Williamsburg - 25 | Breakfast - 26 | Salty Ember - 27 | Lagoon Dwellers - 28

Tributaries -29

Transmissionary Position - 31 | In Law - 33 | Sky Spider (Sermon 6) - 35 | 8 Minute Abs - 37 | Sunset at Kinneret - 38 | Bone of August - 40 | Apple Pie Moan - 41 | Gravedigger - 43 | Amidah I - 44 | Tribe Pride - 46 | Bear Hunt - 47 | Amidah II - 48 | Drifting Off - 49

Throwing Bones - 51

Windy City - 53 | Replica City Ballet - 54 | Mourning Orchard - 55 | Amidah III - 56 | Second Chances - 59 | San Bernardino Line - 60 | Shipwrecked - 61 | Volare - 62 | Blood Guitar (Sermon 7) - 64 | Heinz Hwy 57 - 65 | Harvest Moon - 66 | Amidah IV - 67 | Evacuated II - 68 | Throwing Bones - 69

Bone River Hymnal - 71

Orbituary - 73 | Fog Warning - 74 | Thunder over Louis Armstrong - 75 | Candlelight Lounge - 77 | Blessing - 78 | Number One Hits - 79 | My River (Sermon 3) - 80 | Amidah V - 81 | Lumber Mill - 83 | Bone River Hymnal - 84

Delta - 87

Talisman - 89 | The Recoil (Rural Route 9) - 90 | Amidah VI - 92 | Before the Gun - 94 | Gravesinger (Sermon 9) - 95 | Chain Gang - 97 | Amidah VII - 98 | Sólo Tengo Una Hora (Sermon 11) - 100 | Amidah VIII - 103 | Dangle - 105 | May - 106 | Ambient Murder - 108 | Tomi mi Mano - 110 | Afterword - 115

Isn't this what becomes of it all—
water, smoke, evaporated bone,
dead rain transfigured in heat?
>   -Eric Elliott
>   "The Graves We Dig"

The ditchdigger eclipses grave
               corpse, and sun
his arms, tied to the shovel
>   -Vincent Cellucci
>   "Ditchdigger"

Bone River

As much as we are
        love   death
            cling to each

                    move through the river

Preacher

Sun down   Bone River   a hatchet and a cassock

        gathered limbs
                a fire on the bank
  parish tucked tight
     Preacher sharpens his blade
                sparks against whetstone
                a final amen horizon

naked he wades
     bony waves   the rattle of dried bamboo

he slices his mouth   curses drip
                  the tide blisters

night rises from the deep
   massive bear   mange and nightmare
        up the shore to a cypress grove

the bear swallows the moon
   it lodges in his throat
   he hacks up a beam
        the stars overheat on desolate country roads

Preacher lifts
   the beam   plunges like a shovel into the ground

        leans into it   turns the earth

    the bear's breath fills the trees

moonbeam on a skeletal hand
    Preacher grips the palm   grasps

                        will not budge

dawn's fingers
    over the horizon
        soon the parish will learn to fear first light
            when dreams must be surrendered
            to the rising tombstone

    that heaves and heaves
        and will not let go

from Preacher's "Final Sermons" found buried with a skeletal hand in a cigar box on the banks of Bone River

Fire Line (Sermon 1)

Trees ablaze
learn how forests flame

                our ancestors
                in the fire line

                              snake boots tapping
                                  to the crackling beat

once something catches fire
it becomes addicted to the burn
                it wanders this world's wind
                                breathing its ashes

Flight Pattern

a flutter of wings the hostel pigeons swarm your laugh
full of suicides pulls me out the window through the
branches the Eiffel Tower sparkling toast Champagne
lights these lips our wings whisper *Je vous aime le meilleur*
covered in feathers blown across the sea

                sundown on the banks
                Willowemoc Creek
                your hair cast by the wind
                each strand a scented fly
                across my belly full of hungry trout

alluring blue notes on the Blue Ridge
        Pulaski skyway   flooring your curves

a semi drifts into our lane we skid out of our skin
        off the side of a cliff into a bird
our fingers interlaced feathers our breath our wings

                        in freefall we molt

    and you become They
    and They get on a plane
    and They take off for Indiana or India
    and I become an old man
    who becomes Saturday nights
        standing at the terminal window

    wondering how flight became
                    a nest of broken wings

Like Gravity

Those defiant steps away
    her voice
            naked
       singularity

Newton and Haley
say God used comets
to create the world
       these tussled sheets
             all we need
             to signal
             the end of our kind

she breaks dishes   stretches taut

        across eleven dimensions

     collapsing monuments

        embrace
           our stillborn void

3:08 a.m., Haifa

An open window   holding vigil
I am young   arrayed in dark

>I have no bed no desire to rest
>no mop to wash the moon
>no bucket to bail out the sea

no lullaby
to soothe the volcano
my father lives his final dreams
       ash thrown at stars
       dust over sea

Still the moonlight tugs the tides of his chest
whispering cool lies across the fever's tears

Still the earth embraces fault lines
             as if our bones were never hollow

Stanford C. Lee

Sundown run east
rise west
two dry riverbeds
crib death
match flame
two wet fingers
burning wick
you sit on your back porch
banyan tree oak tree
olive or spruce
drink and smoke
witness
begin

Vidalia

Once more into flood
                Bone River's rusted tide
             peels the onion earth
             washes it away in water-logged chunks

I haven't been this drenched since hiking the Alps

     just another
           rainstorm

                      a ghost
                          tracking memories
            along the Austrian border

     sixty-seven years ago
     the same wilderness
     swallows my grandfather

never given a taste of sweet Vidalia
                 he hated onions
                 his father would bite them as apples
                       exhale onto his face

                    burnt shrub
                        crackling whisper
            in the fireplace of the hutte

descend the mountain
no answers set in stone

The Commute

This day a song
wasted on the deaf
our bones   rusted avenues

cracked sign   the rising moon
       a boomerang hurled
across black tarmac

the sky   that melted road
who are you in this accord?
growing up in the back seat
firework skies   easy freeway
pedal to
oil slicks   bitter fumes
wait and watch the   sky darkened
                silent   the same
                    rumpled suit
          weary eyes
   waiting for the compass to swing

Evacuated

embraced
under the eye of swirling sheets
                tomorrow she flies north
           my arms insufficient anchors

 crescent wounds

shatter-blast
            adrift

foreign shores
       unburied by the sea

outside
Atlanta braces the sky

                      orphans nurse
                        on the haunted
gloss of neon signs

                  echoing reminders

                a sunken city

            outbound spinning flight

from Preacher's "Final Sermons" found buried with a skeletal hand in a cigar box on the banks of Bone River

Ramona's Spiders (Sermon 8)

House asleep in kerosene
spiders hatch in Ramona's ear
        webs cast
        bottles across the broken yard
                August descends bloody fists
                        The Chin & Easy
   toss fire in the loft above Boudreaux & Thibodeaux's
        dry forest in the juke crackling wind
      carry me to New Orleans'
sky   naked at the window Death strangles   stray dogs
        in the sewers rot
        goddamned
        downpour of light
                airmailed fangs
                              postmarked "sun"

Waterborn

   for Ryan and Kate

Silent cloud
        white owl
          perched
        on the mountaintop
        mist drops to earth
           a stream's caress
             turns rock to feathers
                 waterborn   in a valley we
                          your tributaries
             carry the river of you
                     as one through the harvest
           cities that gleam like dew
             countless grains
     on the shore
        given to sea
  the surf gliding
                white owls
             over mountaintops

Terminal Three

gate C10
flight delay
    Preacher's got the gin
        second linin' down the moving walkway

        back home
        his affair with the unrequited
                shallow grave
                    a cat-eyed loa
who blows him kisses from the middle of Bone River
            but won't come ashore
        no matter the tide
               Preacher sings
    baby, your love is watching snow
    pile up outside the terminal window

C16
The Chin
        keeps escape plans in pill bottles
            around his neck
                glowing Muse's heart   sang blue
            drowned in vodka
            took the whole bloody city with it

when it learned the name Em and her new beau
                            gave his child

mayday in the lounge
    Easy's holding pattern over the remains
        a gallon of whiskey

    father's grip   a childhood home
      open wounds

these three

    black boxes   desperate for impact

    believe they're seeing dreams come true
      when they crash the river

        and dance all night in the rubble

Bring Me My Heart on New Year's Eve

the myth of loneliness in new york is no myth this
morning clear blue for the first time in days i hunt gray
skies pillow-talk earl grey & leftovers in the folds of
the blanket we shared two days ago it was snowing
sirens & construction crews were birds today this empty
apartment bare feet on slick wood & bathroom tile only
a fading dream embraces my torso the sweater i wore
last night when i left you at the bar in manhattan with
your friend you held tight & kissed me five times on the
cheek i would marry this sweater if i could even though
right now a breeze colder than gusts on 92nd street
blows through the fabric i cannot stop writing love
poems about escaping row houses hacked up limbs face
to face our interlaced hands pulling us through the
surface of a lake i leave for virginia today & these
empty palms are too small to carry my heart

Williamsburg

Dreams cast
candle lit corners
out over the sun
              tri-cornered cottonmouth
      charmed by Rockefeller

summer's compound fracture

           cobblestone legs

                    cracked and rusted stocks
                  by the crossroad in moonlight

Breakfast

hunger at the end of the bed
        end of fences
        end of the road
    a fire
we have come to expect
                rising sun
                falling stars
                              tombstones in the sky
                                  our dreams
                                  on the cast iron
            split yolk and fatback
                    bloated dawn
                    dream eater
                          tosses us scraps
                and picks the gristle out of its teeth

Salty Ember

   for Christopher Shipman

Sunset's Dalén light
        floating upon the ocean   liquid mercury

        through the lens
        yesterday's shipwrecks cloud the sky
                wash ashore

the Earth holds her heat

    eyes trained on the coming dark

        who pulls the sea with steady hands

Lagoon Dwellers

Belief in each other
blankets our eyes
       puts them on a gondola
       pushes them off our four-post piazza

                lashes to lashes
                    they drift
        through canals of discarded clothes
        poled along with a slurred barcarolle

m'ama, si m'ama,
lo vedo, lo vedo!

our ears have run off with our lips
        and morning shivers our skin
           a city of bridges
            each wave of tongue
                    our treasure

Venice upon tide
this hungry horizon

        our fingertips -
        fishermen
                casting nets at dawn

TRIBUTARIES

Transmissionary Position

Under Virginia's trees
cicadas suckle
        hatch
    screaming drone in the sky
  moist crunch underfoot
        oh god the sweet smell

it's recess and a storm is coming
Mohon and I perch on the eyestalks of the yellow bug
    strange air rooted in the current
        electricity we climb
          down the legs and into our time
      machine position
      arms wide palms up
          spinning loose gravel
the pale underbelly of leaves
calling the rain

Leith and his family are gunned down in their home
    my friend shot in the back
    trying to climb out the window

we are thousands of miles from America and my father
    is dying
Meningitis has taken his mind and he does not know
          his loved ones
         in separate rooms

      quarantined for death

my grandfather has just lost his wife and children to the
         camp
    his parents his brothers sisters cousins everyone else
             in his escape party
             he is alone in the woods
                  shot through the hand

                    alarm drone sky
                          bloodhounds at his heels
             oh god the sweet smell

I've spent all day collecting Memory's caterpillars
                  burnt char
                       in a blue Maxwell House can

                            you should be warned

but capsized I'm sinking
             to the bottom of the Potomac

                       River a bloody lip

                       dark eyes in my stars

In Law

Antlers scraped clean
against the bark of the sky
the trees at her father's farm
lower their crowns
in winter's glycerin
breeze numb face
I slide on borrowed boots
two sizes too big
over frost-crippled grass
the barn the two of them built
on a field of January crows
we hitch the snow-glossed trailer
and I follow his tracks
his daughter on the mount
hugging my waist
we cross the field
at the fallen tree
she leaves me
and runs to help her father
I try to back the tractor and trailer
to the felled wooden buck
in my bones the farmer
gives way to the hunter
I abandon the tractor
and take hold of the axe
cantilevered deep in the tree
her father lifts
in front of her
the wheels spin

we dig our heels
into the earth
butting heads
against the ancient

from Preacher's "Final Sermons" found buried with a skeletal hand in a cigar box on the banks of Bone River

Sky Spider (Sermon 6)

I curse the sun
    orb weaver
        crouched   center web
            nothing but a thief

        steal my rivers
            suck me to a brittle crop

dusty wind   my hair
        stampeding buffalo
            bring on the native
            bring on the hunt
    no lullaby coos like a 12-gauge in my ear

I cover my feet in glass and dance

        naked in the killing field
           naked in the willow

            toss me to the dead

        my lashes fill graves
           fingers worm the earth

by the city on the banks of Bone River
a colony of spiders came ashore with dawn

    tomorrow we will all be pretty silk tombs

8 Minute Abs

Morning routine chugging along the levee warm tombstone in our face November's shitty leaves that's it grow out our hair one last time learn how to say goodbye remember we asked Jon what he would be if anything and Jon said "16" well there we are behind a row of townhouses clear June night but she is 18 and tells us look, *you are still a virgin or whatever okay* pulls up her pants brushes off the dirt *he'll be gone 'til August we should do this all summer hurry up put your dick away we should get back to the party* now let's lean into the wind backwards to the game at Parkview when our knee caved in and Coach Randazzo helped us limp off the field *chin up boy* look at those tall cheerleaders on the sideline waving their branches

Sunset at Kinneret

For showing too much leg
to the nuns, we were branded
indecent and shooed away
from the Church of the Beatitudes.

We retreated down the hill
to the desert-side of Galilee
where we watched the sun leave
footprints in the sea.

For trespassing after hours
we were chased off the beach,
across the water to Tiberias,
where streetlamps outshined starlight.

We plunged off the scratchy turf
into the water in the back of a café,
concrete slabs rose like steeples
above of the slurping ripples of waves.

We swam while two men smoked cigarettes
and sipped vodka under the pinup girls
on strings of beer ads flapping
to the radio's taqsim on an oud.

The water was dark and warm,
and when no one else was looking,
rats ambled down the concrete slabs
and dipped into the water.

Floating on my back for awhile,
my skin began to wrinkle.
I thought of sickle sharp teeth
and searched the sky for stars.

Bones of August

cloud   become thunder
                    damp breeze
                dune grass

ocean spray
        kiss
            blue crab
                pinch

eyes on the half-shell

    scent of sunscreen

        Old Bay tongue

          rum & coke

      lips like
rain on your back

                      wet low-rider jeans

              a salty drop

           sliding your thigh

Apple Pie Moan

The train hasn't run since the hurricane
                    I walk the tracks

    beneath the tide
sweat and trash   stagnant water
              laps against refrigerators
                          tombstones up & down the block

              Louisiana bakes
              I climb the levee's crust
                      rise above bubbling rot
I need to sink my teeth in to what simmers beneath
                                  the drooling sun
                                Bone River sheds
                        her dirty banks
                  one leg at a time

go down your street   lined with pyres
                        these were your trees

I used to be happy with a whiff of apple pie
                            cooling in your window

once you wiped the rim of the plate
and let me lick the juice off your finger
                        the scent on my breath lasted all day

    I reach your house   darkness to a dark eye
                        the last rays of twilight
                                empty sill

                        I sit beneath the edge and wait
               while night falls on the back of my neck
the rising moon slices the sky

       all around me   hungry strays begin to howl

Gravedigger

The flower I carry turns the mossy earth
                      out of her nightshirt
                            grip the stem
                            bend pistil to work

    misted lips hum a requiem
              come for me
              broken ground

      here lie   all the bones we need
                      to tussle the bed

    moonbeam
    blossom of light
    undress dew

irises and poppies
        white lily

        reveal the depths
            of your grave
        become the roots

    let me fill you with eulogies

        give me your tombstone
            let me chisel my name

Amidah I

Abandoned cattle car down by the levee,
                               frosted in Autumn's blood.

Ami raises his hood and leaps from the corroded door
tagged with the fading names of night ferry passengers.

                 He makes his way once again
                       to my grandfather's home.

     Trawling down Bone River's bank
                       like a barge,
      Ami's bowed hood gathers the darkness
                           of rusty predawn.

            In his left hand, leather satchel,
            his right,
                     nestled in his coat pocket,
                     calloused fingers sliding along
                         the rough face of a file.

My grandfather Samuel sleeps
as his old friend follows the overgrown tracks

                     swamp grass
                  browning underfoot,

                             broken bones
                             to his back door.

Every morning,
Ami journeys to breakfast with my grandfather.

Their meal the same:
        black coffee, small pastry,
            toast on Sunday.

    They sit at the kitchen table,
                eat in silence.
Every morning,
  Ami stands behind Samuel,
     cradles his old friend's head in his hands,
      and gently tilting back Samuel's frosted crown,
     Ami files my grandfather's teeth,
                one by one.
When he is finished,
   Ami takes an ancient, dog-eared book
    out of his satchel,
   and together they read the names
       scrawled across yellowed pages
           as the sun
           rises over Bone River,
                flooding the land.

Tribe Pride

Ignore Virginia's sinews

covered with stubble
foot upon the gas

my mother dead
somewhere over the Atlantic

reborn
unfamiliar dawn
over a Paris street

I lose all cardinal directions

cannibal to these stars I am
a treeless mountain lake
the air thin and crisp

Bear Hunt

Stale cigarettes
red flannel
        early morning cross
        the path of the black cat
                wind
                      dark hand   outstretched
      fast fingers fiddle
    like ballrooms on fire

the parish's back roads
                look up to the hunter
                  up to the bull
                        a vertigo of prayer
                    like Spanish moss
              misty sky
              a bear stalked by dawn
          the hunter
plucks a child
iced like king cake
        on the corner stool
                end of the bar
                    a kitchen full of cutlery
                        loves only open mouths
                            dinner bells
        bloodhounds   in the distance
  follow the tracks

            deep in the woods
            death suckles
                      her nipples like rusted nails

Amidah II

When he arrives, Ami stops at the foot of the stairs
to my grandfather's porch,
and looks out across the unkempt field,

broken bayonets, bloody corpses
stretching back to the levee.

A single egret soars over the treetops
on the far side,
dives for the river.

Ami casts prayers like lures.

He ascends the three
cracked wooden stairs
and silently lets himself in.

Drifting Off
   for Wendy

My thumbs
across your shoulders
two white birds
take flight

moon above the lake
nestled against my shoreline

evening stars
through the cypress
your waves
become the sky

Windy City

The Green Mill spins like roulette
                          crimson trumpet
                                charcoal drums

I've come all the way from New Orleans
      for Al Capone's gin

                simple order:
                      7 fingers flashed twice
                      to the tattooed waitress
            her laugh steeped in Seagram's
cold floor   our heartbeats loose pills
                           rolling across the tile
                          this night an empty bottle

one day
      all these lovers
             drown in Lake Michigan

            and we are free
            to sing about the butter dish at The Drake
            and the price of a ticket to the Bulls game

thus elevated   the grave
                  rumbles overhead
                  while we circle the Rosebud
                  in the rain
                          looking for a parking spot

Replica City Ballet

Once our bed
    now plastic rose

        thorn & petal

          empty song

            painted desert
            atop an atrium

              a dusty ceiling fan
          swirls dunes
          down avenues   city lights

              our stars

                  Bedouin fires

                distant drums

Mourning Orchard

Late summer night
        low against Bone River
                stars like lanterns

      floating downstream

           the coming
           harvest of ashes

lights on the far side await the ferry

    come ashore

        in the orchard
        the moon tends the rows

      tributaries
           familial pyres
              filled with bones
    the wind we breathe
   against the stones
moonlight casts her silver pieces
           across the potter's field
Bronze John dances
                tomb to tomb
            the widows hover

    mosquitoes around the porch light

                  waiting to feed

Amidah III

My grandfather first met Ami in the fields
    on the outskirts of his village-

  Samuel, just a boy, crouched under smoke
                           wafting over wheat.

      His mother and siblings behind him
        hidden in dark woods
        with some of the villagers.
  Unable to take his eyes off
      the tower of fire, Samuel's father
      is held down by Sol and Jacob,
      who do their best to silence his rage.

  Above my grandfather,   no stars, no moon.
                            Only smoke,

                his father's curses.

Samuel crawls through the fields
                in the darkness
                    toward the fire.
                    Silhouettes of Russian soldiers
                    bowed in roaring flame.

Shhhh.
The sound
        from over his shoulder.

Behind him in the wheat, a thin boy.
>   Hooded, flickering light,
>   >   he was thirteen,
>   >   he was sixty,
>   >   he held a thin finger to thin lips.

>   Hunkered amongst the sheaves,
>   the boy writes in an old leather book
>   >   with an old file like a quill, dipped in blood.

Samuel crawls toward him.

>   >   "Can I see?"

"No. Not yet."
>   The boy closes
>   the book.
>   >   "When it's finished?"

"It won't be."
>   >   Samuel faces the fire—
>   >   searing embrace around the collapsing frame.

Ashes to ashes.

>   "My home."

The boy does not look up.
"There will be others."

>   >   He slides the book into a leather satchel,
>   >   >   the file into his pocket.
>   >   He settles beside Samuel.

They stare into the inferno.

Ashes from ashes.
"Make of this a home."

Second Chances

cemetery spread eagle
like Starlet's
pill bottle eyes
        the moon
        a nurse's uniform

                      latex fingers
                      dripping needle

        vacant ground
                a question

                calling her tombstone
                      from the foot of the stair

San Bernardino Line

Left in the back lot
    farthest corner
  where chain links meet
  by the tracks

    your ambulance

        trapped at the crossing
          we are reflected

            windows of passing trains
                flashing lights

              emergencies on hold

what can be done
waiting on the rising arm of the sky to move us

Shipwrecked

Naked in the storm
this creaky porch
    a shotgun's rotting leg
                      lists in the current
        the earth's black magic

so hold the splintered post

press your face into the downpour

    palm trees possess wind

    slow lightning ambles across sky
                      delicate tentacles

a jellyfish overhead   oblivious
                we are his wake

                marooned reverberations
                    sinking into sludge

Volare

Somewhere south of Lecce
                a blue medusa
    the Adriatic turns
          time to stone
    beneath the sky's broken shield

    an island of ruins

    crumbling look-out tower
            I stare at the sea
                shimmering hair
                brushing the shore

    I ask only to be wind
        gliding through its long strands
    my fingers
      lacerated limestone and salt
    shrivel in the sun

  absent of skin

overflow
        horizon's nets
  ever receding
                circles of birds above
                    soft feathers
                    simple prayers

        leap from the cliff
plunge into the sea

    float silently to the bottom

                an embrace
      the ruins know best

from Preacher's "Final Sermons" found buried with a skeletal hand in a cigar box on the banks of Bone River

Blood Guitar (Sermon 7)

We could be the wind at the edge of a meadow
fingering sweet grass stars fishin' the river hotshots
chillin' at the Chevron down the street candy shell
spinners wood-grain dash topless given to the bass
given to the twitters I've always been one for hundred
spokes and slow cruising windowless summer nights
breath in your ear nibble this lobe come roll a pinner or
two and let's cruise the back roads cut out your heart
and fling it at the next person you see the world
revolves in the woods behind the library Songbird
Jenny lost her virginity to the Grateful Dead on the 4th
of July love cannot save us we cannot be saved so we
love our grand finale sets off all the alarms in the
parking lot

Being Hwy 57
for Jeffrey Miller

I am so American
I will die eating hotdogs
on the Fourth of July

I've been to the North
and it is called **"We Thank You
For Not Smoking"**

out west the Califortunate
pick up streets like butts
or UCLA Cheerleaders

dust off the altar tops

the choir warms up

in the cemetery

God looms like debt

around the corner
from the town square

greasy burger joint

dive bar

exit ramp

Harvest Moon

for Frank Stanford

Through bare branches
the stars scatter
flickering whitetails
in the black forest
the hunter watches
behind an ivory pipe
passed from father
to father
to son the rifle
takes aim
two deep drags
from the belly
deep in the mountains
the ashes stir

Amidah IV

Ami enters the kitchen silently,
 slides off his hood,
   lays his satchel on the table,
       and pokes his head into the bedroom.

       Samuel sleeps in a nest of threadbare sheets.

       Ami stares at his friend. How old
       he has become, his face,
                withered flame.

   Not much longer now.

Evacuated II

Under cover of night
we chart a path
    miles from dreams

    we have in common

        this windshield
        the coming storm

            broken levee

                      our witness

                Mississippi stars

                      speak our end

Throwing Bones

Day and night
    game of double-six
    between the sun and moon
        dawn's handshake
                a stack of bills
                    C-note top
                  I-O-U's beneath
            the notches
        on our tombstones
        double-zeros

      spinning back
        into the line of play
    stars and clouds
          empty hands
          scattered across the bone yard

BONE RIVER HYMNAL

Orbituary

Arc of shore sand
    above the gravediggers' kids
    shattered horizon
       speckled egg
       fallen from nest
          castles poured into the sea
                  ancient aviary
                              echoes
                        crest the surface
              feathered waves
                      beating   beating

Fog Warning

Autumn sun set
a mountain pyre
       we are Appalachia smoke
            the sky
                  slick with ghee

        headlights tumble
        over the guardrail

           under streetlamp halos
           wait our children
           in their scars

    night's breath swirling soma

we lick the flames embossed on whiskey bottles

      ashes dancing on the back of slow tongues
                              revolving

Thunder over Louis Armstrong

Big Easy sick
genius I am
November's blues

        snowflakes riffing
        trees knobbed bones
        sunset lit with southward wings

then Sunday gray
    rain stumbling drunk

Monday   a perfect apocalypse
      our heads are skyscrapers
      to the clouds that hustle over
      the jackknifed truck
          pink insulation snow on I-10

now there is thunder over Louis Armstrong
       another cold front pounds the stockyard

  all planes grounded

  New Orleans cannot leave
      the waves
      her nature
      this song

    my apology

        I am done with November
            and it ain't even all souls'

I should catch tropical dewdrops
through the sunroof
day-dream
        Tabasco on every corner
                the banyan bow of her eye-lids

or I could honk
at the altar boy on Carrollton
        swinging change buckets
        and waving forgiveness
                to all the passing cars

Candlelight Lounge

Louisiana eats its weight in strippers' dreams

                no camera flashes
                    hairy knuckles

Candi panties become Bone River
        drifting through a barren field

nothing left at the state fair but slow-spinning clouds

        underneath this rusty carousel
        lovers learn the true stakes of the Ring Toss

                tattered bassinet in the dumpster
                fallen nest aflame

fuck the blue bird
        if he pecks your head
            slide under the garage door
                chop that motherfucker right in two

this time of year
        Preacher hangs a bony hand around his neck
and starts showing up at the Candlelight

these are the notes
        he whistles to his gin

Blessing

Let us pray

at the bar
everyone plays guitar

& they all play Iron Maiden

what can we know

pink French nipples
under the Eiffel Tower

my mausoleum of gin

a monument so hideous
I pass out

every crumb
the bouncer sweeps out the door

Number One Hits

Our situation one more pop song our flag burns the day
a dusty diamond inside our bones sprout leaves and gust
through the land where girls wear boy's pick-ups like
original sin Easy's shattered mirror shows links break
chains only the strong survive free after the fireworks
Death reclines on his back porch inhaling spent
gunpowder like the world's last cigarette while his ears
rifle through the hum of air conditioners for the
churning dark river where wind will not die.

from Preacher's "Final Sermons" found buried with a skeletal hand in a cigar box on the banks of Bone River

My River (Sermon 3)

The moon slips off the horizon
calls me to your bed
                      dwindling puddle
                          how sickly I've been
                              stagnant and receding
                                  since last rain
                  under the bastard sun I burn
            breach the levee
                call your waters home
                feed your currents
                      swallow me in your tide
       I kneel on the shore   become your waves
    spread muddy legs
        and I wade in
                grab me by the throat   take me under
                on the banks
                the whole world turns to dust
    I'm done with land   I cannot walk
            and done with air   I will not breathe
                  pin me below and roll your waters
              teach me to live
                        a creature of your deep

Amidah V

The cattle car rumbles towards Belzec.

    My grandfather searches the icy metal wall for breath
                                    in small drafts,
        momentary relief from the stench,
            stale piss and fear

                rolling off the dark
                woolen coats pressed against him,
  wayward prayers,
    minyan
  swaying in the dark train.

    Not neighbors, not friends, family-
        lost in the wail of the upland
            back across the Polish border.
    The names of those never to be
                      held again.
No angels wrestle here.
No prophets'
   empty promise of Heaven,
      of Hell.

    At the foot of this ladder,
        night's shattered crystal.

        Cast on the other side,
                the sun's hollow resurrection
        steps over corpses.

Ami makes his way to my grandfather's side.
Samuel grabs him, holds him tight.

His head buried in Ami's hood, my grandfather
  sheds the tears he could not find in the wheat,
    in the ghetto,
      at the station.

      His wife and children,
      November's final, pale leaves,
        torn bare from his branches
        by the icy breeze.

    "My family."

Ami runs thin fingers through Samuel's thinning hair.
"There will be others."
My grandfather sobs, a deep, ancient sound.

    The two sink to the floor.

  Ami reaches into his satchel,
    removes the book—
      thick leather binding,
      yellowed pages like vellum.

Through the holes corroded in the side of the train,
  dawn's searchlights illuminate the names
    scrawled on page after page,
      the names cast upon the walls of the cattle car
        from the dark woolen coats.

"Come,
we must read them."

Lumber Mill

we awake as a city

   covered in bark

      our leafy dreams

         tumble out the sky

            scaled and decked

               timber down the flume

                  the sun a spinning blade

Bone River Hymnal

The Wind buys the river
shots of Patrón
    for this
    ghost train city
        rusted tracks   rumbling night
          dirty and wailing
              mother long gone

Jay Cat's by Circle K
      sunk in the swamp
     corner bar   gators circle
          stale bait in the windows
   gang initiation
       tonight
       three women'll be shot
           don't worry   a hoax
             only *fais do do*
       strip off your skin
      stretch it over the bayou
whittle them bones   beat on them drums

        Bone River takes us as Bone River does

  Death rides a street cruiser all night
through the Bottoms
       better change color
         slink 'long the fence
        eat insectual   elongated tongue

Spring's comin'
nature's money shot   up in your nose
                                            all over your hair
                                            coating your car

       evening sun slips off   the sky   dirty condom

shaking off old man's grip
Easy rises with the trees
                    blossoming mouth
                                     rotten leaves
     back from father's tomb

         gossamer shades come to cross
                 in the light of the train
   down by the levee   how many graves
and Bone River takes us as Bone River does

each day   cane fires   blown from the west
          redden the eye   tighten the throat
         feel the bubbles   beneath your skin

           the end of Western Civilization
The Chin pops a bottle and sets up shop
leans out the window to the passing parade
                     he sings
                             feliz extinction
          everything in the pot

     Tony Chachere's cauliflower
        potatoes corn and sausage

Toothless Thibs builds a fire outside his front door
        sucks fresh strawberries   juice on his chin

                      the kettle boils

    Tee Loc's Harley butchers river road

  savage and drunk
the river got on Shippy and he couldn't shake it loose
      cracks and crumbles   his mud face
          dark fish skulk and snap underneath

    this is the land falling into the sea
    this is the land falling into the sea

Preacher sits on the levee
    and plays his harp to the river
        calling each wave closer to shore

    hear the whistle blow

  feel these currents flow 'round the bayonet
        stuck deep in a corpse
                this land
a thousand notes   one song
      inked on Aly's left foot   state map
          overlaid with switchblade

      three drops of blood

    and Bone River takes us
        as Bone River does

DELTA

Talisman

When the old lady screams a million prayers take flight in the heads of the sunbathers turning to Jesus Christ I didn't see you there I knew I would never make it to you in time I open a hundred beers from New Orleans to Venice and back on Frenchman born suicide how to tell mother & father you're here right now a sacrifice where we meet at the pyre of this word flutter the pages dark beast behind dreams
                       graves
                                   uniforms

The Recoil (Rural Route 9)

                lightning stumbles home from the bar
        searching the sky for keys
      Preacher by the window
      sermons to the tv
          crosses on the side   Rural Route 9
                                      my commute
                                      in clouds
                  chiseled headstones
puddles in the parking lot
            feed the fog like blood
                    the river goes nowhere I cannot
        believe
        these shackles are free
                    curtains clasped together
              trying to remember something of light
slept all day yesterday
all day tonight
    one last throw-down
    at the speakeasy
                Moongoddess kisses
    we get drunk and the river calls me a pussy

    The Chin tosses a chair against the wall
                            outside
      Shippy's drunk   himself   a nose for blood
  his heartbeats cigarette butts   suicide off the porch

downstairs Big Country's layin' rails
            for the Southern Pacific
      another 6 a.m. and the Sun'll tap his window

      can't sleep here

           run down River Road
                dawn to sun   hound to hunter
        fast on our trail
    nowhere to hide
Easy's shotgun
        double-barreled chrome-osome
         somewhere between Texas and Bone River
    you'll find his motel room

do everything you can   his finger's on the trigger

          one light burns over the empty levee
   on the banks
   a rising bird

        on the wind
        the recoil

Amidah VI

Samuel mutters in his sleep.

Ami glances back at his satchel,
    feels the weight of the book inside,
            the burden, etched

        deep in his shoulder,
            the nerves webbing his muscles,
                  whisper an endless roll call.

He shakes his head once
and lays out their breakfast.

    As he fills the kettle, Ami stares

            out the kitchen window:

                    dawn's hemorrhage.

Sirens fill the sky.

> Samuel is deep in the woods,
> bloody hand stuffed into tears,
> > a filthy, striped uniform.

German shepherds
> at his heels,
> > blood-soaked earth.

A thin hand grabs him by the shoulder,
rips off what's left of the camp's clothes.

> Ami stuffs Samuel's uniform into his satchel,
> covers him in mud and rotting leaves.

"Your new scent."

> > The corpses
> > of all he knew.

Ami lifts the skeleton of his old friend
and carries him far from the searchlight,
> far from the coming
> > curse of dawn.

Before the Gun

Before dawn's light cracks
    the speckled egg
before the horizon
      splits yolk from morning

New Orleans' alleyways spill mist
     foreign to the pines of Georgia
        the pines of Vermont
        the pines of Rome
    but not pine boxes

ballrooms and bars
sing a requiem
    before the last dream fades
    before the rising alarms
    before the people drown
        one last chance
          to return night's embrace
              hands clasped
                before first light
                longing for the gun

from Preacher's "Final Sermons" found buried with a skeletal hand in a cigar box on the banks of Bone River

Gravesinger (Sermon 9)

Born Preacher
              singing graves
                          don't believe
                          the sun's rays
                                    reign without clouds
                      retrovirus   sky
            eats us top to bottom   inside out
                          white blood stars burn
                        universal crop

sunshine and lightning   call and response

   every day the levee lies and would see us drown
        in dawn's wave   we are forgotten dreams
   I wake with a mouthful of jellyfish
bobbing just below the surface
       the gulf is dying   we feed it more land
               what has become of the delta
               what has become of our child
burning sky
the warning far   and farther away
               tombstones twinkle in the night
      sickness to their own
           solar complexes

      bend over your barren nest
                every dawn   lashes back
          every dream turned against you
          every wing stitched to earth

            nothing from over the tree-line but fire

we would desert if only the Sun had its way
a withered husk   a skeletal hand
I sing you   grave dreams
            a lullaby floating in the murk
                    tentacles on the breeze stinging
    your eyes are hookers   the light their pimp
it's sunrise
    get on your knees   get on your knees and take it

Chain Gang

orange sundown tattered jumpsuit horizon barbed wire
cool nights cold bottles jailbreak by the overpass
Preacher slangs po'boys like amens the day's debts
settle by night in the gravel lot under the freeway
skinned knees chalky dust shattered whiskey bottle the
stars shoot snake eyes and shuffle off down the alley
behind the Happy Note Easy breaks his thumbs stuffs
'em in his eyes this swamp city of bridges burnt bones
can't outrun long arm of the soul have mercy on the
moon a knife hilt deep the fog rolls off Bone River
the last bluesman in this town an undead moan shuffles
along the levee trying to recall the words

Amidah VII

Deep in the cave
under a host of trees—

>   in Samuel's hand,
>   the bullet.

"Bite down."

>   Ami slides a coarse file between
>   Samuel's chapped lips,
>   rotting gums.

Even muffled,
    the scream echoes
        the black depths tunneled below.

    Ami chucks the bullet into the darkness.

"Now we burn your clothes."

>   Frozen since the train,
>   Samuel's tears melt once more,
>   soft sobs sliding down the stalactites,
>   gaunt cave,
>   his face.

>   My grandfather's eyes before the fire,
>   his wife and children,
>   before the night,
>   his brothers and sisters,
>   eyes before
>   his mother, his father.

All he knew in corpses.

"This world."

Ami tosses the tattered uniform onto the flames,
                  embraces my grandfather.

"There will
be others."

                  Ami removes the old book,
                  Samuel's blood
                  stains the cover.

"Come,
we will write the names."
        Ami's thin fingers grip Samuel's,

    guide the bloody tip of the file

            across the pages,

                the corpses
            of all he knew

    stare into the dark cavern.

"Make of this a home."

from Preacher's "Final Sermons" found buried with a skeletal hand in a cigar box on the banks of Bone River

Sólo Tengo Una Hora (Sermon 11)

años pasaron	years passed
siguen los cuerpos	the bodies still
aqui temblando	trembling here
tome la sangre	it takes the blood
comi el cuerpo	commissions the body
mis lagrimas	my tears
quiebra el espejo	bankruptcy mirror

-Cedric Bixler-Zavala, "L'Via L'Viaquez"

on the other side of that window
        missionaries on Mars
                bathe in soot
                    cum on the furniture
      got no soles
      gnaw feet to the bone
    every night grind   eyeteeth to blindness
                good investment
                    eat shit anyway
      sólo tengo una hora

    chainsaws dream orchards
        the sun   a rotting peach

smolders on Futureman's desk
      burnt holes in his wooden head
                on the wall above

Bolaño's been smoking the same cigarette
            since October

                    sun   rise the end of days
                            no volume loud enough
                            no color too sharp
                        a razor stepping
                    Bone River high
                            against the ashen levee
                    smokestacks refine their howl

Marinette spreads bony wings
over her delta   overflowing wax
        wolves with flaming tongues
            swim inside
                            where's the jimson
                                where is Bondye
                                sólo tengo una hora
                                        homeless

filthy wind knocks on your window   no spare change

gust shattered glass

                        bloody hands in your hair
                            how much you gonna give now

                    how many fingers around your throat
                    how many fingers around your throat
                                sólo tengo una hora

be ready   the sun's in town
                        Savage Detectives on the run
        Pamplona Santa Theresa

        Santa Theresa Cuidad Juarez
      who is the princess   who the bait
                     who my friend
                     the charging bull
    better run
    beat a retreat to a beachside bar
                     thatched roof
      Corazon   dark amulet
    full of knives
  tome los cuchillos
      lángelos en la corona

or pistols at dawn
    walk outside
        the sun pisses
              and you smile

              umbilical horizon
                  cut this cancer loose
  2012 and heads will roll

      down the stairs into the den
      midnight family around the furnace
      still getting off to the scent of dawn
breathe it in
breathe it in
breathe it in
breathe it in

Amidah VIII

Ami stares out my grandfather's
kitchen window.

He knows what is to come—

even the softest dawn
        kills the frost,
                drops of dew
                sliding down blades of grass.

From the back room,
        dark cave of sleep,
      gentle sobs startle Ami.

He hesitates at the window.

    Outside, halfway between the house and the levee
      an egret lands on an oaken bough,
          bloody fish in its beak.

Ami turns to the table
and opens the book.

                Blank page.

                              He raises his hood,

            turns back to the widow,
            and takes the kettle off the stove.

With great care, Ami slides
the file from his pocket,

            and heats it in the flame.

Dangle
for Vincent

    them Cederdale cats
dig nine graves to fill
        America's supermarket
      lives forever in the heart
        strange photo albums
        dawn   day   dusk
        inscrutable tattoos
            poisoned alley cats   wailing
                  by the motel pool
                  Walt Whitman drinks
          head back   massive beard
              entangled wings
              filling the sky
        stench of chlorine
      matted tufts of fur
            it's not your fault

      The Chin and his mother ghost
          the banks of Bone River
                cut each nother's hair
    behind Eli's Guest House

    moon swept clippings

        the tide white owls circle

    the distance between sand and glass

May

Roll down windows
forget how to brake

turn the song up
all the way
ten thousand roadside blossoms

accelerando of newborn summer
dust crowding your rearview
riding your ass and blowing horns

over the shoulder
rebirth dies
in the stifling arms of warmer winds

the earth's bedding billows
each shake airs out the season

storms churn above

our traffic patterns
        tail-lit explosions
          a serpent devouring

those who obey the speed limit
break the rules of the road

we can end right here
our arms encircle
more than the wheel

accelerate!

Leave with cymbals crashing

        the season on full volume

Ambient Murder

Enough of this shit
Easy, load the shotgun
                    -Preacher

Churning thighs

rise from the rubble

Red Stick Savings & Loan

I push off the banks

   tomorrow's New Year

      a crime I aim to see

   stylized rusty honky-tonks

      oscillating jukes

         armed with every national anthem

            only a matter of time

         before we come to

         over a cocktail napkin

         pray the moon remains

sunlit tombstone

tossed hatchet

open ground

Tomi mi Mano

Sunrise　　　　　Bone River
　　　　　　　　　a hatchet and a covenant

　　　　　　　empty pit
　　　　　　　　　ashes on the bank
　　birds take flight
　　　　　　　　　Preacher sharpens his blade
　　　　　　　　　　　sparks against whetstone
　　　　　　　　　　　a requiem horizon
naked he wades
　　　　　　　bony waves
　　　　　　　　　　　the rattle of dried bamboo

he slices his wrist　　　his hand drops
　　　　　　　　　　　　　the tide whispers
　　come　　　　*come*　　　　*come*

night　　slinks to the deep
　　　　　　emaciated bear
　　　　　　　mange and nightmare
　　　　　　　　down the shore from a cypress grove
through the parish's back roads
　　Death's black Mustang swerves over the yellow line
　　　　　squealing tires
　　　　　　　　　break lights
　　　　　　　　　　　　the pines fill with blood
　　　　　　　the rising sun
　　　　　swallows the bear
　　　　　　　　　　he lodges in its throat
　　　　　　　　　　it hacks up a dream

                    a dawn with no sun
                 to drown the stars
             like rushing water

Preacher lifts
         the dream   bloody wrist
                       dead hand   cigar box
                                 bottom of the pit

                      veil of fog off the shore
Preacher's vows fill the trees

                     the last shooting star
                               kisses the river

sunbeam   a skeletal hand
                     'round Preacher's neck
     dawns fingers
                     'round the Parish's throat

                          the sky sounds the alarm
         first light
         a hole in the earth

              Preacher bows to the river
                           fills his mouth
    he sinks to his knees
          the wind like dried rice against his shoulders

                 morning bells peal

O river   my river
*   I sing   your song*
*   your waves*
*   my chest*

*   heave and heave*
*   and never let go.*

AFTERWORD

Upanisad

The soul of this book
    the world's holy breath
    its body sky,
    paper mountain,
    its belly the earth
        beneath our feet.

 Walk its day and night,
      these poems, just seasons
      these pages—clouds,
      these letters—stars.

  You are the day placed in front of the word
  I am the night placed behind.
    Together a pyre,
      pleading for a spark,
        our tongues a song of fire.

      Harmony's tinder,
     we are smoke rising
        between words,
     thunderheads
     over our ashes.

In the beginning
there was nothing here at all

Benjamin S. Lowenkron's home is the river. Born and raised in Virginia by the Potomac, he moved beside the James and the York to attend the College of William and Mary, and he now lives with the Mississippi in Louisiana where he received his MFA from LSU and teaches at Baton Rouge Community College.

www.ingramcontent.com/pod-product-compliance
Lightning Source LLC
Chambersburg PA
CBHW020902020526
44112CB00052B/1190